Preface

The ability to prepare and deliver a professional presentation is likely to prove invaluable to pupils throughout their school and later careers. Microsoft PowerPoint is a leading graphics package for use in designing presentations to be delivered either using a computer and large screen or with the aid of an overhead projector. PowerPoint presentations can be designed and delivered on any subject right across the curriculum, and this book is packed with ideas for different topics and styles of presentation. At the same time, pupils will be developing their confidence and skills in the use of ICT for communication in a most enjoyable and satisfying way.

Teachers of pupils in all age groups from 10 upwards will appreciate the straightforward manner in which the capabilities of PowerPoint are explained. Pupils will find they are able to design their own presentations after only a few lessons and will enjoy impressing their audience with amazing special effects!

Basic PowerPoint 2000 is suitable for whole class, group and individual teaching. It will also be extremely useful to show teachers of all subjects who are new to ICT how to use this software and it will give them the confidence to use it in class successfully. Teachers are likely to find it useful both for delivering their own presentations to classes and for helping pupils become equally proficient.

The purpose of this accompanying teacher's book is to

 aid in lesson preparation;

 give extra information to teachers on some more advanced topics;

 supply photocopiable worksheets to reinforce what has been learned and to test understanding.

The photocopiable sheets in this book are suitable for using away from the keyboard, and answers to all the questions will be found in the back of the book. A record sheet and a Certificate of Achievement are included.

Microsoft PowerPoint 2000 is used in all the examples, but schools using a different version of PowerPoint will have little difficulty adapting to minor differences in the screenshots, toolbars and menu commands.

Copies of each example presentation used in the chapters are available for downloading from our web site www.payne-gallway.co.uk

Robert Heathcote

Contents

Introduction

ICT in the curriculum

ICT is now recognised as a separate subject within the National Curriculum. Schools organise and deliver the curriculum in different ways, with ICT sometimes being delivered as a separate subject, and sometimes as part of a cross-curricular scheme. Whichever approach is taken, pupils cannot progress unless they are introduced to the capabilities of the various software packages they are expected to use. A number of lessons needs to be devoted to allowing pupils to acquire the necessary skills, before they are asked to put them into practice in a subject context across the curriculum. This series of books is designed to assist teachers in imparting these essential basic skills in a straightforward but entertaining and lively manner.

Lesson planning

Each chapter in this book is designed to accompany the corresponding chapter in **Basic PowerPoint 2000.** It provides a summary of the learning objectives of each chapter and some advice on any preparation required before the chapter is taught in a classroom. Possible pitfalls are pointed out, and extra tips given where these are likely to be useful.

Teachers may find that a single chapter takes more than one lesson, especially if time on the computer is limited. Extra tasks appropriate to a particular year group and area of the curriculum can be set so that presentations can be planned away from the computer.

The worksheets

These will be invaluable both to reinforce skills already encountered, and as part of the learning process. They are constructed so that they can be completed away from the computer, and so that a minimum of marking is required on the part of the teacher. Answers to all questions are given in the back of the book.

Record sheet

Successful completion of the worksheets will provide clear evidence that topics have been mastered, and a record sheet is provided at the end of the book so that each pupil can keep a record of the worksheets completed.

Working at home

Many parents may want to purchase books in this series for their sons and daughters to use at home – or for that matter, to use themselves! Most people enjoy being 'tested' on what they have learned and the worksheets will give much satisfaction in this respect. Although **Basic PowerPoint 2000,** for which this is the companion text, is primarily aimed at pupils from year 5 upwards, people outside this age range – aged 8 to 80 – will appreciate the straightforward, simple and effective approach to learning the ins and outs of presentations with Microsoft PowerPoint.

Chapter 1

The Basics

Learning Objectives

▶ To load PowerPoint.

▶ To name and identify the Title bar, Main Menu bar and Standard toolbar.

▶ To use the AutoContent Wizard to create a simple presentation.

▶ To type and replace text.

▶ To identify the Outline View.

▶ To view a slide show.

▶ To delete slides.

▶ To save a presentation.

▶ To close a file.

New terms and vocabulary

Graphics presentation package, Title bar, Main Menu, Standard toolbar, Status bar, dialogue box, slide, Normal View, Slide Show, Presentation window, icon, Escape, highlight, drag, delete, file, extension, save, close.

Resources needed

A computer loaded with **Microsoft PowerPoint** (preferably one for each pupil), photocopiable sheets marked Sheet 1a and Sheet 1b (Extension work).

Preparation

Photocopy Sheets 1a and 1b for each pupil. If there are not enough computers available, pupils could work in pairs or you can draw up a rota to show them the running order for computer access. The worksheets can be completed away from the computer.

Pupils can spend extra time designing a presentation of their own appropriate to one of their curriculum subjects.

You will need to make sure that you have a suitable folder (i.e. area on disk) on each computer or on the network ready to save the pupils' work.

What to do

Go through the lesson first with the class, demonstrating how to load PowerPoint and start the AutoContent Wizard.

Explain how to view a slide show after it has been designed. To do this, click **Slide Show, View Show** from the main menu or click the **Slide Show** button in the bottom left-hand corner of the window. It is one of a group of very useful icons which will be used frequently to change between different views of a presentation during design work.

Allowing the pointer to rest for a few seconds over an icon will bring up a Tool Tip giving its name.

Give out the first worksheet (Sheet 1a). Extension Sheet 1b can be used as an extra activity.

Sheet 1a **The Basics**
(Classwork)

Name: _____ Date: _____

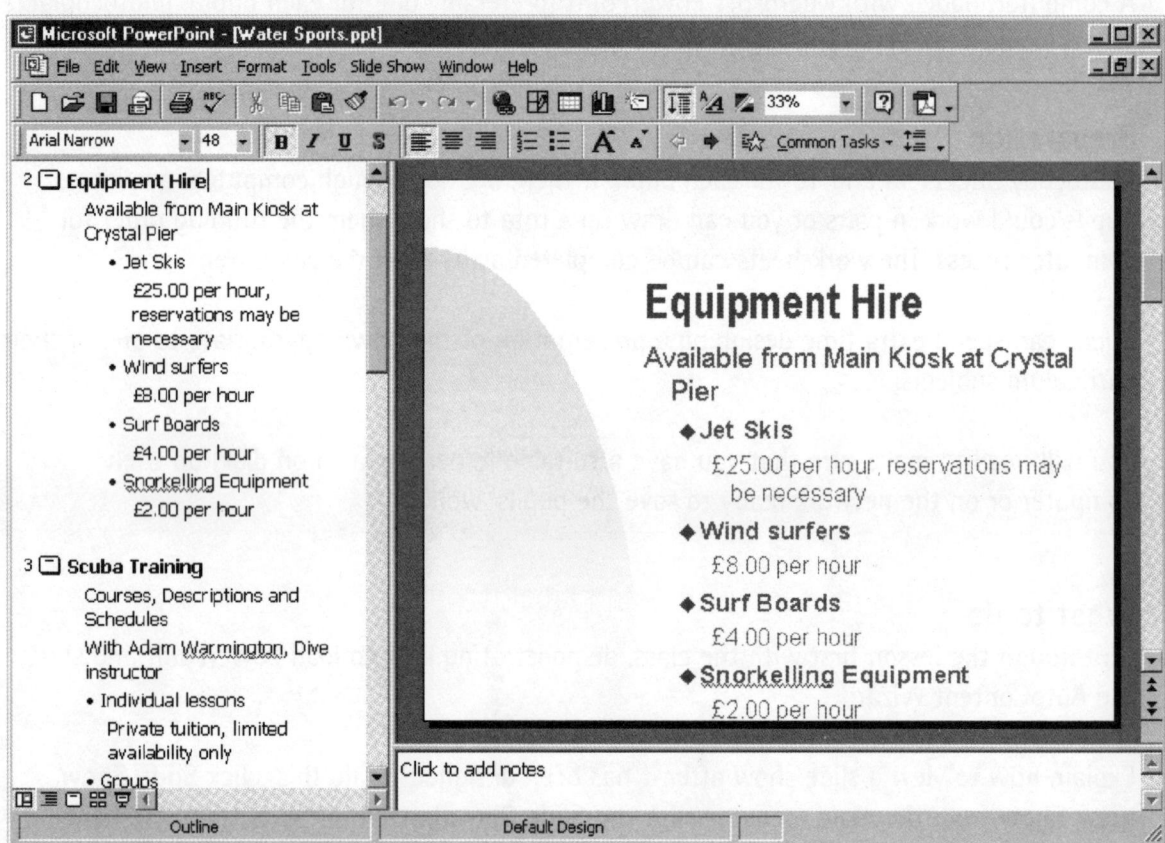

1 Colour the Formatting toolbar red and label it **1.**

_____

2 What is the heading text of Slide **2?**

Answer: _____

_____

3 How would you select Slides 2 and 3?

Answer: _____

_____

4 Suppose you wanted to delete these slides. How would you do that?

Answer: _____

_____

5 Draw a border around the presentation window in the screen shot above and label it with a **5**.

6 Which slide is shown in the presentation window?

Answer: _____

_____

7 Circle the slide icon for slide 3 and label it with a **7.**

8 Look in the **Status** bar at the bottom of the screen.
Which view is currently on the screen?

Answer: _____

_____

9 Which option on the Main Menu bar will you choose to save a document?

Answer: _____

and then _____

_____

10 Circle the Slide Show icon and label it with a 10.

Sheet 1b **The Basics**

(Extension work)

Name: _____ Date: _____

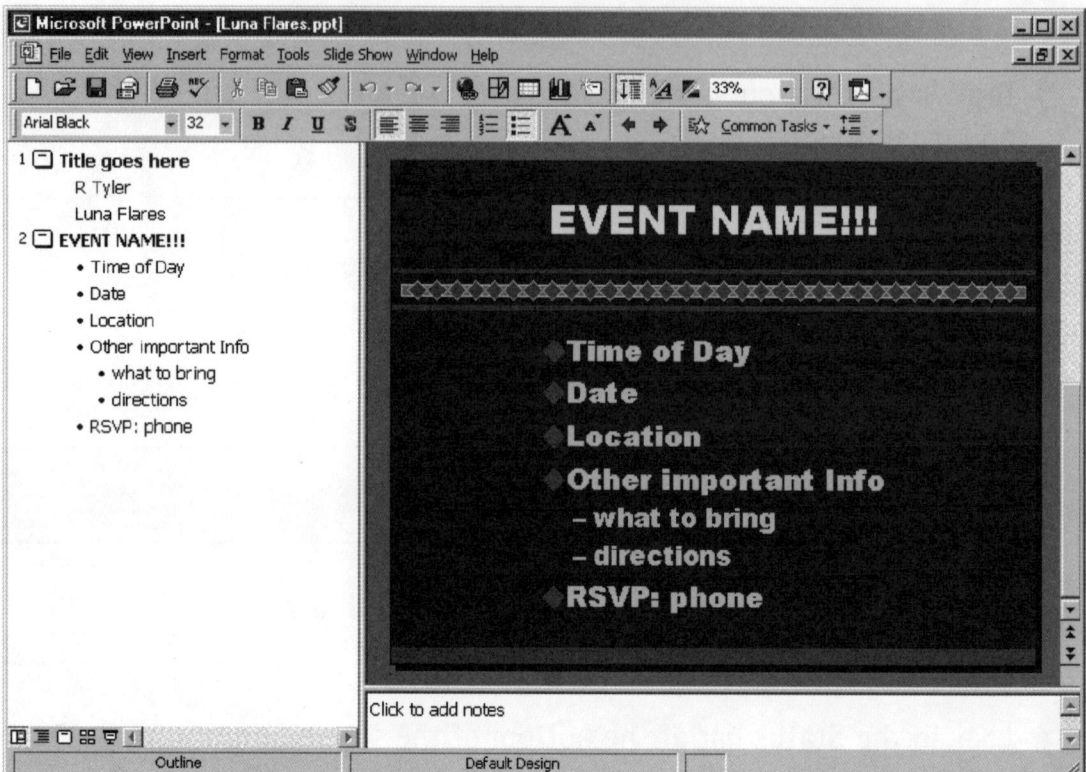

1 What is the right hand window pane called?

Answer: _____

_____

2 What three letters has **Microsoft PowerPoint** automatically added to the file name that was given to this document? Circle and label with a **2** the part of the screenshot that gave you the answer.

Answer: _____

_____

3 What view of the presentation is shown in the screenshot?

4 Change the title of Slide 2 to **Moonwalk** on the screenshot.

---

5 The pointer changes shape when you can edit text. Draw this shape in the box below.

Answer:

---

6 How would you insert an extra line before **Time of Day** on Slide 2?

Answer: _____

---

7 What is the file name of this presentation?

Answer: _____ . ppt

---

8 Circle the button you would press to view the slide show and label it **8**.

---

9 Which key on the keyboard would you use to stop a slide show before it reaches the end?

Answer: _____

---

10 Ring and label with a **10**, the icon you would click to save your presentation.

Chapter 2

Template Wizard

Learning Objectives

▶ To plan a presentation.

▶ To use the Template Wizard to create a presentation.

▶ To design a title screen.

▶ To format text and move it around the screen.

▶ To change the view.

▶ To begin a project.

New terms and vocabulary
Animation, Template Wizard, AutoLayout, sub-title, formatting, text box, Slide View, Slide Sorter View, Notes Page View.

Preparation
Photocopy Sheet 2a, Sheet 2b (Extension work) for each pupil. The worksheets can be completed away from the computer.

What to do
Demonstrate how to create a new presentation using the template option. Note that the method will be slightly different depending on whether you are loading PowerPoint from scratch or have it already running.

Students may like to look at the different presentation designs available. (See figure 2.2 of pupil's book.) You should encourage them to use them to use the recommended **Capsules.pot** for the purposes of this exercise.

Point out that they will be using different layouts (see figure 2.3 of pupil's book) for each slide. Explain what a placeholder is.

Be sure that they understand the difference between selecting a box and selecting text within a box. (See figure 2.5.) If the box is selected, formatting will apply to all text within the box, but to format or edit just part of the text, the words themselves need to be highlighted by first clicking inside the box.

Give out the first worksheet (Sheet 2a). Sheet 2b (Extension work) can be used as an extra activity.

Sheet 2a **Template Wizard**
(Classwork)

Name: _____ **Date:** _____

1 Give one tip on how to design a good presentation.

Answer: _____

_____

2 How would you insert a title in the slide above?

Answer: _____

_____

3 Draw the button that you would click to centre the line.

Answer:

_____

4 Suppose you have entered a sub-title already.
How would you move the sub-title text box around the screen?

Answer: _____

5 Which **view** of the slide is shown in the screenshot above?

Answer: _____

6 How would you change to **Slide Sorter** View?

Answer: _____

7 Draw the button you would click to view the slide show.

Answer: [ ]

8 Which shortcut key would you press on the keyboard to end a slide show?

Answer: The _____ key.

9 Look in the status bar at the bottom of the screen in the picture. Which template is being used in this presentation?

Answer: _____ pot

10 Why should you save your work regularly?

Answer: _____

_____

_____

Sheet 2b **Template Wizard**
(Extension work)

Name: _____ Date: _____

1 Circle some text that has been **centred** and label it with a 1.

---

2 How many slides are there in this presentation?

Answer: There are _____ slides.

---

3 Suppose you want to make some text **Italic.** What should you do before selecting the correct button from the **Formatting** toolbar?

Answer: _____ the text to be changed,

or: select the _____ .

---

4 How do you select a line of text.

Answer: _____

---

5 Which **Slide Layout** do you think is being used for the slide in the picture?

Answer: _____

6 Suggest 2 factors in designing a presentation that can help make it more effective.

Answer 1: _____

Answer 2: _____

Look at the pictures below and answer questions 7–10.

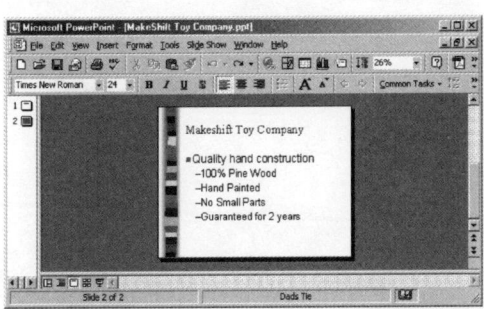
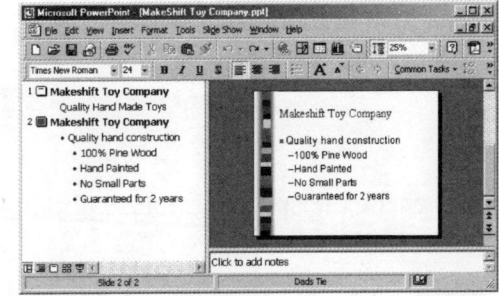
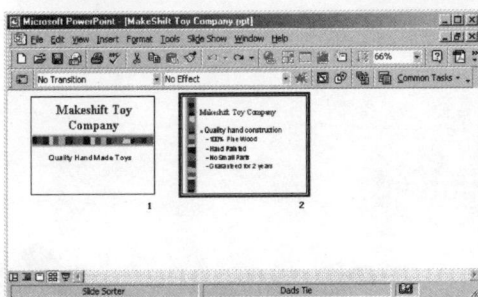

7 Label the screen in **Slide Sorter View.**

8 Label the screen in **Slide View.**

9 Label the screen in **Outline View.**

10 Which slide is currently displayed in the Presentation window in the centre picture?

Answer: Slide number _____

Chapter 3
Editing a Show

Learning Objectives

To open an existing presentation.

To change the font size.

To check the spelling of presentation slides.

To insert new slides.

To change bullet styles.

To move text around and change the order of slides.

New terms and vocabulary
Bullets, font (text style), Tab key, demote, promote.

Preparation
Photocopy Sheet 3a, Sheet 3b (Extension work) for each pupil. The worksheets can be completed away from the computer.

Note that the presentation as it was at the end of chapter 2 is available to download from the Payne-Gallway web site (www.payne-gallway.co.uk). You can download this and save it in your own folder prior to the lesson. It can then be copied to individual pupil folders if required. This can be useful if some students have lost their presentations or wish to come back to this chapter at a later date and go over some of the earlier techniques.

What to do
Show how to open an existing presentation bearing in mind the differences in this task depending on whether or not PowerPoint is already running.

Point out the Outlining toolbar which is normally 'docked' down the left hand side of the screen. The **Promote** and **Demote** buttons are on this toolbar. Toolbars can be displayed or hidden using the menu option **View, Toolbars.**

Give out the first worksheet (Sheet 3a). Sheet 3b (Extension work) can be used as an extra activity.

Sheet 3a **Editing a Show**
(Classwork)

Name: _____ Date: _____

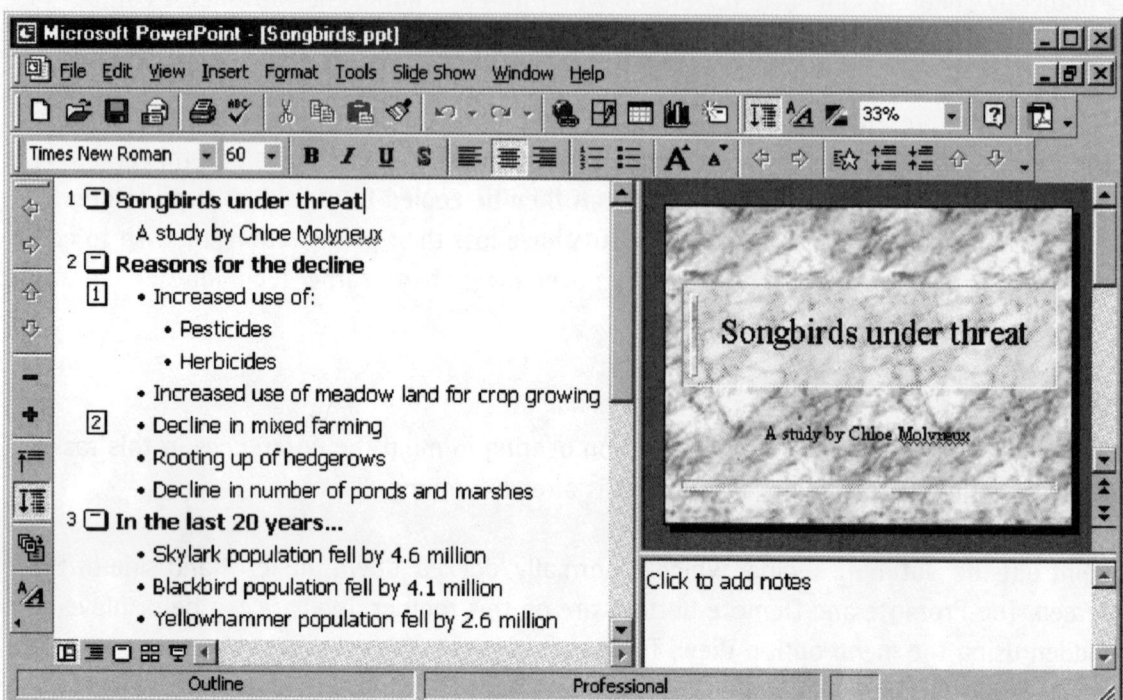

1 How would you increase the text size of the title in Slide1?
Circle the button you would press and label it with a **1**.

_____

2 Which view is the above screenshot showing?

Answer: _____

_____

3 Circle and label with a **3**, the button you would press to check the spelling in your presentation.

_____

4 Which icon would you click to select all of the text on Slide 3?

Answer: The _ _ _ _ _ icon.

5 Describe how you would move Slide 2 below Slide 3.

Answer: _____

_____

6 Circle and label with a **6**, the button you would press to insert a new slide.

7 Circle and label with a **7**, the button you would press to indent the selected lines in the picture below.

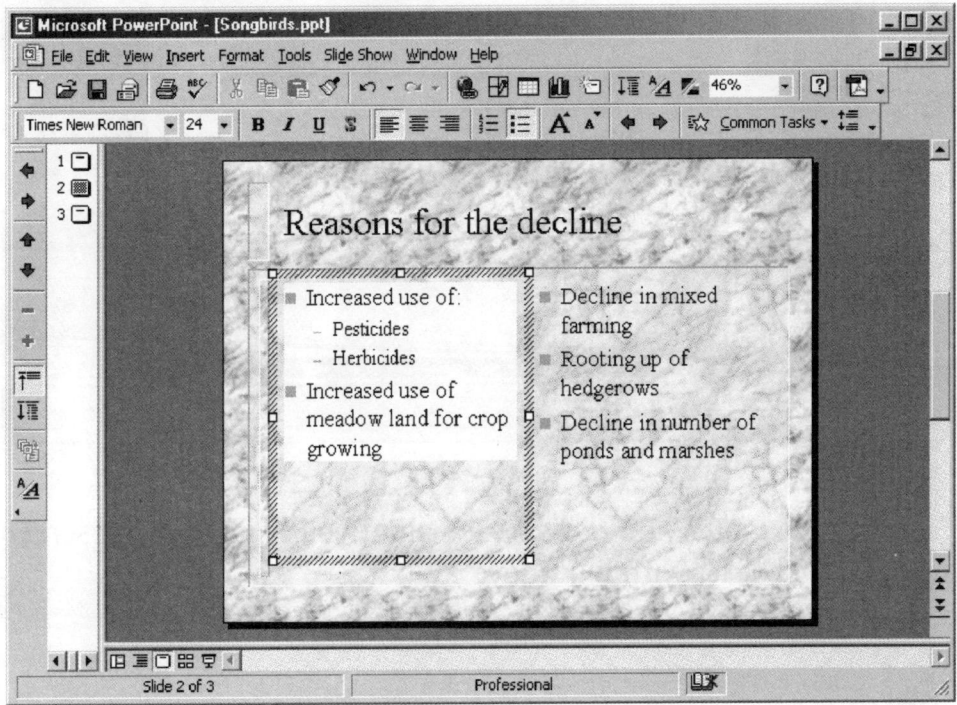

8 What are the little squares next to each line called?

Answer: _____

9 Which menu options would you use to change the appearance of these little squares?

Answer: __ __ __ __ __ __ __/__ __ __ __ __ __ __ ...

10 Circle and label with a **10**, the area on the screen that tells you which slide you are currently looking at.

Sheet 3b **Editing a Show**
(Extension work)

Name: _____ Date: _____

1 Which button would you press to see all of your slides on the screen at the same time? Label it with a **1** above.

Answer: _____

_____

2 Describe how you would make the heading text bigger.

Answer: _____

_____

3 Which button would you press to view the slide show?
How would you make sure that the show starts at the beginning?

Answer: _____

_____

4 Which Slide Layout is this slide based on?

Answer: _ _ _ _ _ _ _ _ _ _ _ _

5 Which view should you be in to check the spelling of the entire presentation?

Answer: _____

6 Which template design is being used for this presentation?

Answer: _____ .pot

7 Circle and label with a **7**, the button you would press to change to **Outline** View.

8 (a) Label the Outlining Toolbar with an **8**.

(b) How can you display the Outlining Toolbar if it is not visible on the screen?

Answer: (b) _____

_____

9 Explain how you would change the appearance of the bullets used in the slide.

Answer: _____

_____

Chapter **4**

Applying Designs

Learning Objectives

To change the Design Template of a slide.

To change the colour scheme on individual, multiple and all slides.

To change background colours and styles.

To change the layout of a slide.

New terms and vocabulary

Template, gradient, texture, pattern, object, Clip Art.

Preparation

Photocopy Sheet 4a, Sheet 4b (Extension work) for each pupil. The worksheets can be completed away from the computer.

Note that the presentation as it was at the end of chapter 3 is available to download from the Payne-Gallway web site (www.payne-gallway.co.uk). You can download this and save it in your own folder prior to the lesson. It can then be copied to individual pupil folders if required. This can be useful if some students have lost their presentations or wish to come back to this chapter at a later date and go over some of the earlier techniques.

What to do

There is nothing in this chapter that pupils will not be able to follow on their own. Some pupils may have time to try out more advanced features, for example by clicking on the **Custom** tab on the **Color Scheme** dialogue box (Figure 4.2 of pupil's book).

By the end of this chapter, they will probably be ready to start making their own presentations in topics of your choice or theirs!

Give out the first worksheet (Sheet 4a). Sheet 4b (Extension work) can be used as an extra activity.

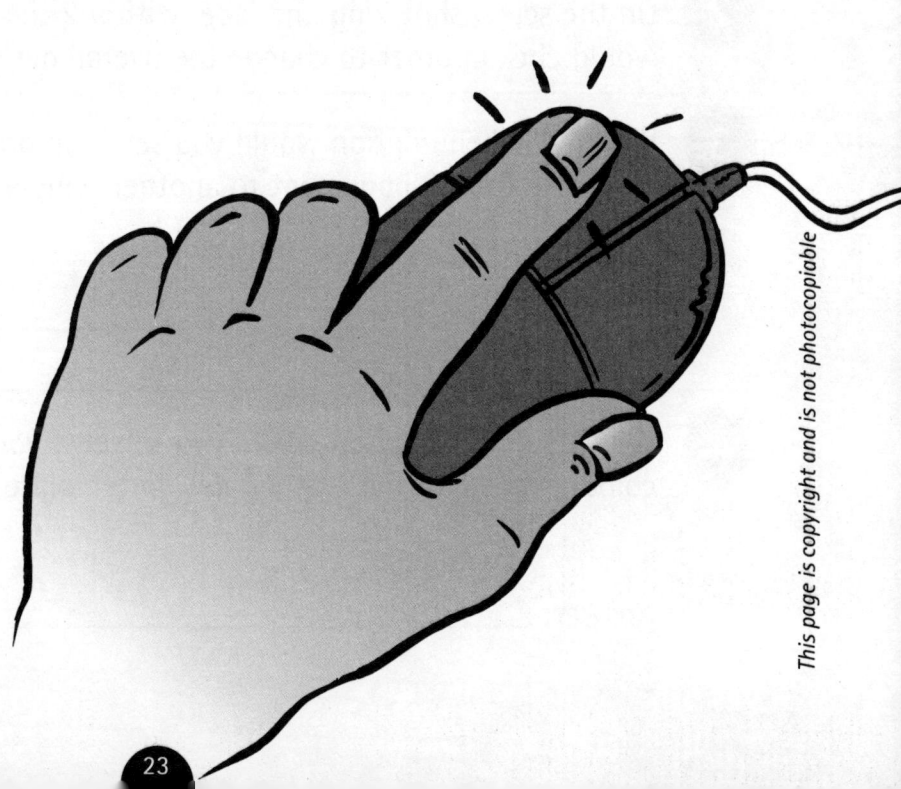

Sheet 4a **Applying Designs**
(Classwork)

Name: _____ Date: _____

1 Which view is the above picture displaying?

Answer: _____

2 On the screenshot, ring and label with a **2** the main menu option that you would click in order to change the overall design of the slide.

3 Which submenu option would you select in order to change the **Design Template** from **Ribbons.pot** to another template?

Answer: _____

4 Which submenu option would you select if you wanted to change the colour scheme of the existing design template?

Answer: _____

5 Explain the difference between the options **Apply** and **Apply to All.**

Answer: _____

_____

6 Which tool would you use to scroll through your slides whilst in **Slide** View?

Answer: The _____ _____ bar.

_____

7 How would you change the font size of the title **Ludwig van Beethoven**?

Answer: _____

_____

_____

8 **PowerPoint** sometimes underlines words with a wavy red line. Why?

Answer: _____

_____

9 Circle and label with a **9,** the button you would press if you wanted to insert a new slide.

_____

10 What is Clip Art?

Answer: _____

_____

Sheet 4b **Applying Designs**

(Extension work)

Name: _____ Date: _____

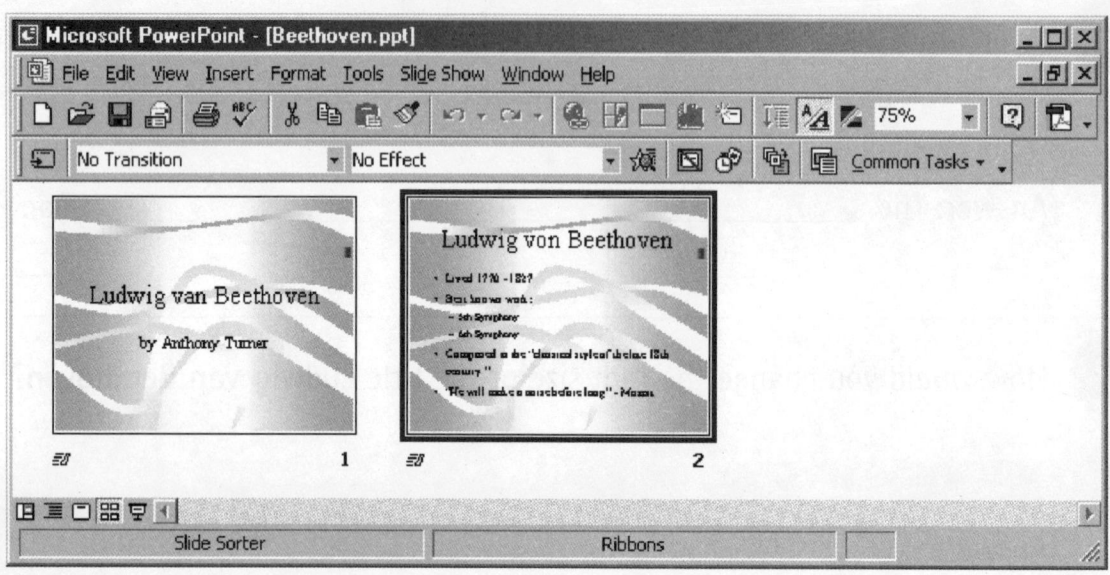

1 Which slide is currently selected?

Answer: Slide _____

_____

2 What would be the effect of double-clicking the first slide with the mouse?

Answer: _____

_____

3 Which option will you select from the **Format** menu (shown below) to add a **Fill Effect** to a slide?

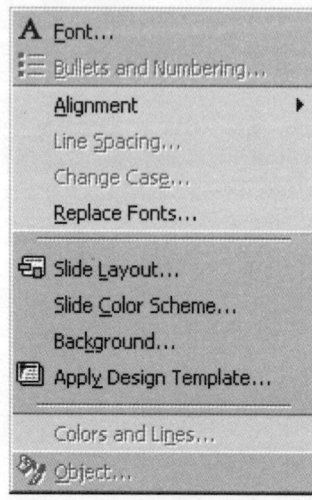

4 Name 2 different **Fill Effects** you could add to a slide background.

Answer: _____

_____

5 How would you change the layout of a slide?

Answer: _____

_____

6 There were 2 *placeholders* on each of the slides shown above.
What is a *placeholder?*

Answer: _____

_____

7 Draw a ring around the button that you would press to view your show.
Label it **7**.

_____

8 Which shortcut key would you press to exit the slide show?

Answer: _____   _____

_____

9 Which shortcut keys would you use to move forwards or backwards during
a show?

Answer: _____   _____

_____

10 How would you delete Slide 2?

Answer: _____

Chapter 5

Adding Objects

Learning Objectives

▶ To change the spacing between the lines of text.

▶ To insert a clip art image.

▶ To resize a graphic without distorting it.

▶ To use the scroll bar to scroll up and down a screen at a time.

▶ To add a chart to a slide.

▶ To change datasheet column widths.

▶ To delete chart data.

▶ To edit a chart.

▶ To move slides.

▶ To erase a bullet from a line of text.

▶ To centre text.

New terms and vocabulary
Object, chart, datasheet, spreadsheet, cell, column header, spacing, handles.

Preparation
Photocopy Sheet 5a (Classwork), Sheet 5b (Extension work) for each pupil. The worksheets can be completed away from the computer.

Note that the presentation as it was at the end of chapter 4 is available to download from the Payne-Gallway web site (www.payne-gallway.co.uk).

If you have any CDs containing clip art you may wish to use these images to insert into the presentation instead of those provided with **MS Office**.

Some knowledge of Excel is going to be helpful both for the teacher and the pupils. Some parts of this chapter are quite complex and it would probably be a good idea to try it out before the lesson to familiarise yourself with the techniques.

What to do
Explain that an object could be, for example, a bulleted list, clip art graphic, photograph, drawing or chart. Any of these can be inserted into a slide. The important thing is to choose an appropriate slide layout first (see Figure 5.6 in the pupil's book). Some layouts allow only text, some allow tables, charts or clip art. If you want to add an object to an existing slide which does not have a placeholder for the object, you should first of all change the slide layout as explained in Chapter 4. (In Outline view select the slide and then select **Format, Slide Layout...** from the main menu bar.)

Give out the first worksheet (Sheet 5a). Sheet 5b (Extension work) can be used as an extra activity.

Sheet 5a **Adding Objects**
(Classwork)

Name: _____ Date: _____

1 How would you demote the last point on the slide?

Answer: _____

_____

2 How would you increase the size of the font in the title?

Answer: _____

3 What is a placeholder? How many do you think there are on this slide layout?

Answer: _____

_____

4 On the screenshot, ring and label with a **4** the **Center Text** button.

5 What would you do to the clip art image placeholder in order to insert a picture?

Answer: _____

6 When you select a graphic, little squares appear on each side of it. What are these little squares called? What are they for ?

Answer: _____

7 How do you change the size of a graphic without changing its proportions?

Answer: _____

Look at the screen above and answer the following questions.

8 Ring and label with an **8**, the slide layouts that will automatically give you a placeholder for some clip art.

9 How many slide layouts will insert a **chart** placeholder on a slide for you?

Answer: _____

10 Why should you save regularly?

Answer: _____

_____

Sheet 5b **Adding Objects**

(Extension work)

Name: _____ Date: _____

1 Which icon would you click to move Slide 2 below Slide 3?

Answer: _____

2 How would you remove the bullet from the fourth point on Slide 2 (Paralyses prey with poison fangs)?

Answer: _____

3 The name **Basnyet** on the first slide is not recognised by the **PowerPoint** dictionary. How would you get rid of the wavy red line **PowerPoint** puts under it?

Answer: _____

4 Which handles on a graphic would you have to use if you wanted to change its size without distorting it?

Answer: _____

5 Circle on the bar below, the button you would press to increase the paragraph spacing between selected lines of text.

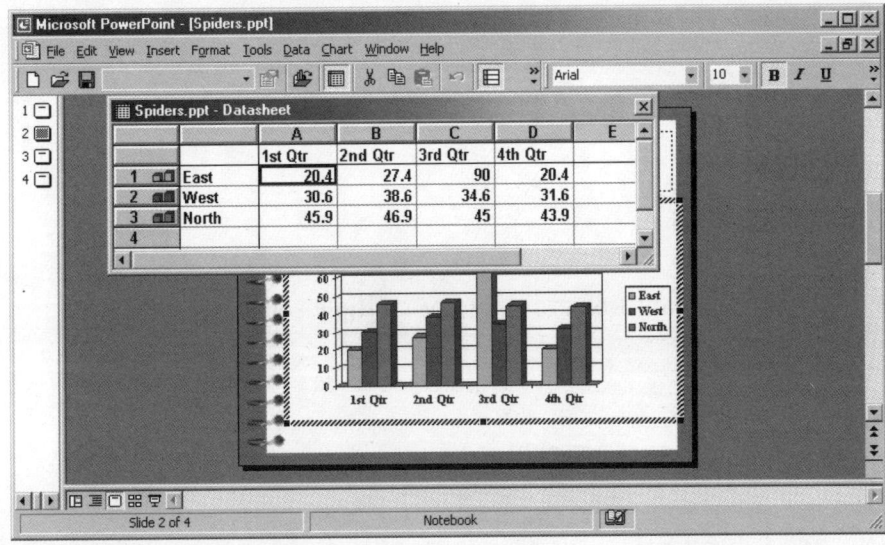

Questions 6 - 10 refer to the picture below.

6 The small window with a table of data is called a datasheet. How would you increase the column widths in the datasheet?

Answer: Drag _____

7 How would you delete one of the columns?

Answer: Click the _____ and press _____

8 Circle and label with an **8**, the button you would press to close the datasheet.

9 Which menu options would you use to reopen the datasheet if you needed to edit the data?

Answer: _____

10 How would you add your own data to the sheet?

Answer: Click in one of the _____ and begin typing.

Chapter 6

Special Effects

Learning Objectives

▶ To add slide transitions to single or multiple slides.

▶ To add sounds to a presentation.

▶ To add special effects.

▶ To animate text.

▶ To animate objects.

New terms and vocabulary
Pop-up menu, transitions, animation.

Preparation
Photocopy Sheet 6a, Sheet 6b (Extension work) for each pupil. The worksheets can be completed away from the computer.

To hear the sounds you will need a sound card installed in your computer and a set of speakers. Without these the sounds inserted as special effects will be unheard, but the pupils can still practice inserting a sound for trying out on a computer with speakers.

Note that the presentation as it was at the end of chapter 5 is available to download from the Payne-Gallway web site (www.payne-gallway.co.uk).

What to do
This is a fun chapter and it would be a good time to suggest some other presentations that would allow pupils to practise techniques and effects learnt so far. Faster pupils could then work on their own presentations in parallel with the text. This also encourages experimentation with the package which is sometimes the best way to learn more, for example some pupils may want to try out the custom animation feature in more depth.

Give out the first worksheet (Sheet 6a). Sheet 6b (Extension work) can be used as an extra activity.

Sheet 6a **Special Effects**
(Classwork)

Name: _____ Date: _____

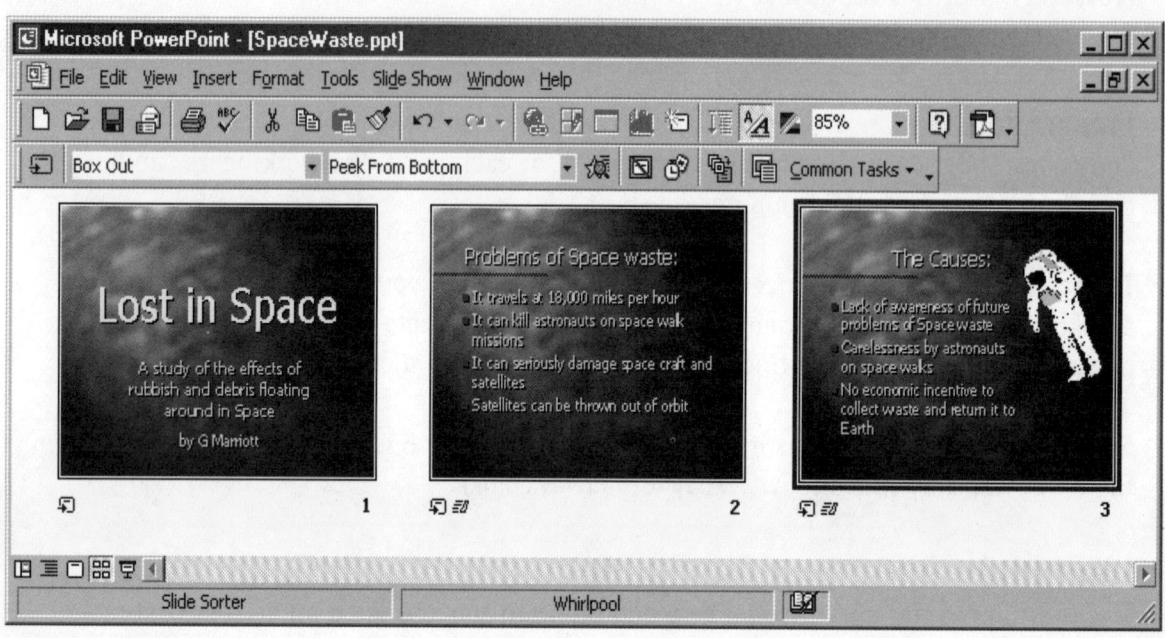

1   Draw the button that you would press to view the slide show.

Answer:

2   What is the shortcut key used to end a slide show?

Answer: The _____ key.

3   What does the small icon underneath Slide 1 represent?

Answer: _____

4 Slide 2 is currently selected. What is the name of the transition it is using? Ring and label with a **4,** the part of the screen that tells you.

Answer: _____

_____

5 Name 2 other transitions that could have been used here.

Answer: _____ _____

6 Describe the **Split Vertical Out** transition.

Answer: _____

_____

7 Draw a border around the **Slide Sorter** toolbar.

8 What does the second icon underneath Slide 2 represent?

Answer: _____

_____

9 Which Effect is the selected slide currently using to animate its text? Ring and label with a **9,** the part of the screen that tells you.

Answer: _____

_____

10 When viewing a slide show, name 2 keys you can press to get the next or previous screens.

Answer: _____ and _____

Sheet 6b **Special Effects**
(Extension work)

Name: _____ Date: _____

1 On the **Slide Sorter** toolbar shown below, ring and label with a **1** the slide transition icon that would bring up the window above.

_____

2 What is the difference in the effects of clicking **Apply** and **Apply to All**?

Answer: _____

_____

_____

_____

3 What is the difference between a *transition* and an *effect*?

Answer: _____

_____

_____

Microsoft PowerPoint - [SpaceWaste.ppt]

File Edit View Insert Format Tools Slide Show Window Help

Box Out   Peek From Bottom   Common Tasks ▾

Lost in Space

A study of the effects of rubbish and debris floating around in Space

by G Marriott

1

Problems of Space waste:
- It travels at 18,000 miles per hour
- It can kill astronauts on space walk missions
- It can seriously damage space craft and satellites
- Satellites can be thrown out of orbit

2

The Causes:
- Lack of awareness of future problems of Space waste
- Carelessness by astronauts on space walks
- No economic incentive to collect waste and return it to Earth

3

Slide Sorter   Whirlpool

---

4 Which slide(s) is/are currently selected?

Answer: _____

_____

5 How do you select more than one slide at the same time?

Answer: _____

_____

_____

6 How many slides are using effects?

Answer: _____

_____

7 Which menu options would you use to add a sound?

Answer: _____ / _____

_____

8 You can animate an object in the same way as text by using the **Custom Animation...** window. **True** or **False**?

Answer: _____

Chapter 7

Show Time!

Learning Objectives

▶ To use the right-hand mouse button with the shortcut menu.

▶ To navigate around a presentation.

▶ To use the freehand pen during a presentation.

▶ To use and print handouts.

▶ To use the Notes Pages.

New terms and vocabulary
Pen, handouts.

Preparation
Photocopy Sheet 7a, Sheet 7b (Extension work) for each pupil. The worksheets can be completed away from the computer.

Note that the presentation as it was at the end of chapter 6 is available to download from the Payne-Gallway web site (www.payne-gallway.co.uk).

What to do
This chapter concentrates on techniques that can be used in a live presentation. Although these work best with a projector connected to the computer and a large screen, there are other quite satisfactory ways of delivering a PowerPoint presentation. For a small audience the computer screen may be quite adequate on its own.

Pupils need to be shown how to sit sideways on to the computer so that they are facing the audience, and to arrange chairs for their audience so that everyone can see the screen. Some students may want to prepare handouts.

The 'pen' tool is a useful device for emphasising a point on the screen. (See figure 7.3 in the pupil's book.)

An alternative method of delivering a presentation is to print out the slides onto transparencies and to project them using an OHP. Delivery techniques are discussed further in chapter 8.

Give out the first worksheet (Sheet 7a). Sheet 7b (Extension work) can be used as an extra activity.

Sheet 7a **Show Time!**
(Classwork)

Name: _____ Date: _____

1 Which mouse button do you need to press in **Slide Show** view to see this menu?

Answer: _____

2 Which 2 menu options let you move forwards and backwards through the presentation?

Answer: _____

3 On the menu, which option is currently selected?

Answer: _____

4 Give one use for the Pen.

Answer: _____

5 How do you activate the Pen?

Answer: Click _____ on the Pop-Up menu

and then choose _____ .

---

6 How would you change the pen colour?

Answer: Click _____ and then choose

P _ _   C _ _ _ _ .

---

7 How would you erase all the pen marks from the screen?

Answer: Click _____ and then choose _____ .

---

8 In which views can you add notes?

Answer: _____

---

9 As a speaker, how would you view your notes during a presentation?

Answer: Click the right mouse button and select _____

_____

---

10 What is the shortcut key to end a show?

Answer: The _____ Key.

Sheet 7b **Show Time!**
(Extension work)

Name: _____ Date: _____

1 Which view is currently visible?

Answer: _____

2 What happens when you click the right-hand mouse button in **Slide Show** view?

Answer: _____

3 Name 3 different colours of Pen that you can have.

Answer: _____ , _____ or _____

4 Look at the menu below. You are currently viewing slide 1.
How would you jump directly to slide 3 using the shortcut menu?

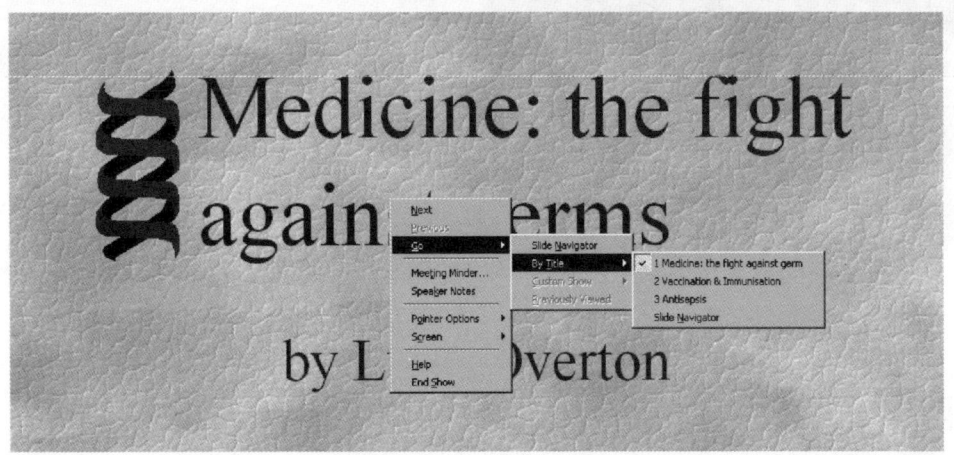

Answer: _____ / _____ / _____

---

5 Give 1 reason for incorporating handouts into your presentation.

Answer: _____

_____

_____

---

6 Label on the picture below where you would click to print the notes pages
or handouts.

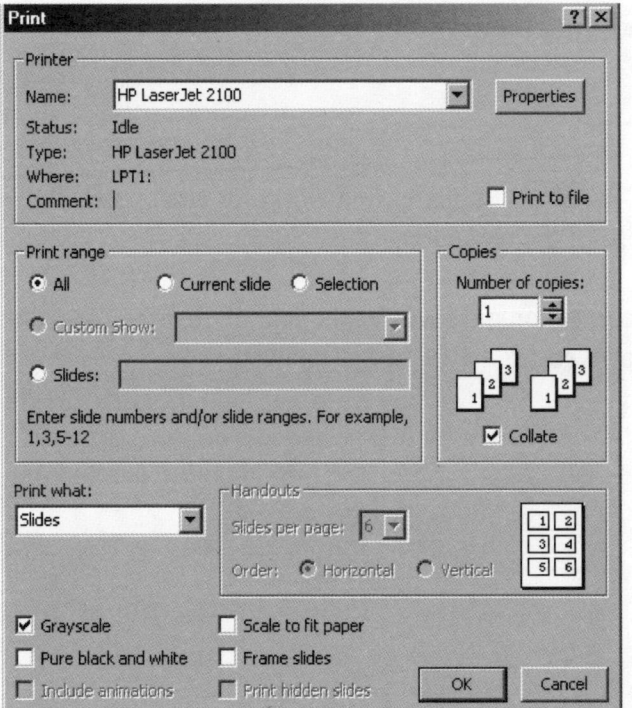

Chapter 8

Delivery

Learning Objectives

▶ To develop good presentation skills.

▶ To set up an effective presentation.

▶ To appreciate the importance of practice and rehearsal.

▶ To interact with the audience.

▶ To produce a self-running kiosk presentation.

New terms and vocabulary
Kiosk, hardware.

Preparation
Photocopy Sheet 8a, Sheet 8b (Extension work) for each pupil. The worksheets can be completed away from the computer.

Note that the presentation as it was at the end of chapter 7 is available to download from the Payne-Gallway web site (www.payne-gallway.co.uk).

What to do

This chapter builds on presentation skills learnt in chapter 7. The only new technique described is how to set up a kiosk presentation. This will run without intervention and will loop until stopped.

There are 2 options which can be checked in the **Set Up Show** dialogue box (see figure 8.3 in the pupil's book):

 Browsed at a kiosk (full screen). Clicking the mouse has no effect in this mode. The presentation loops continuously using timings set up as in figure 8.2.

 Loop continuously until 'Esc'. This causes the slides to loop automatically if timings have been set, otherwise the slides can be advanced manually by clicking the mouse. If timings have been set, the mouse will still override the automatic advance if clicked.

Practical work to accompany this lesson needs to involve pupils in rehearsing and delivering their own presentations.

Give out the first worksheet (Sheet 8a). Sheet 8b (Extension work) can be used as an extra activity.

Sheet 8a **Delivery**
(Classwork)

Name: _____ Date: _____

1 Give one reason why you should rehearse your presentation before going 'live'.

Answer: _____

_____

_____

2 You should rehearse your presentation before delivering it in front of an audience. What else should you do?

Answer: Check the _____

_____

_____

3 Give an example of a good delivery technique to use when facing your audience.

Answer: _____

_____

_____

4 Why should you ask your audience questions during your presentations?

Answer: _____

_____

_____

_____

5 What else can you do to keep your audience involved and attentive?

Answer: _____

_____

_____

_____

6 Why is it not a good idea to provide long handouts just before a presentation?

Answer: _____

_____

_____

_____

Sheet 8b **Delivery**

(Extension work)

Name: _____ **Date:** _____

1 What can you do to your appearance to help increase the impact of your presentation?

Answer: _____

_____

2 What is the main feature of a **kiosk** presentation?

Answer: _____

_____

Look at the screen shot below and answer the following questions about kiosk presentations.

3 Ring and label with a **3**, the button you would click to add a transition to a slide.

_____

4 There are 10 slides in your presentation. How many slides will the transition apply to if you click **Apply?**

Answer: _____

5 Show on the screenshot under question 2, what it would look like if you had decided to make each slide advance automatically after 8 seconds.

Look at the screenshot below and answer the following questions.

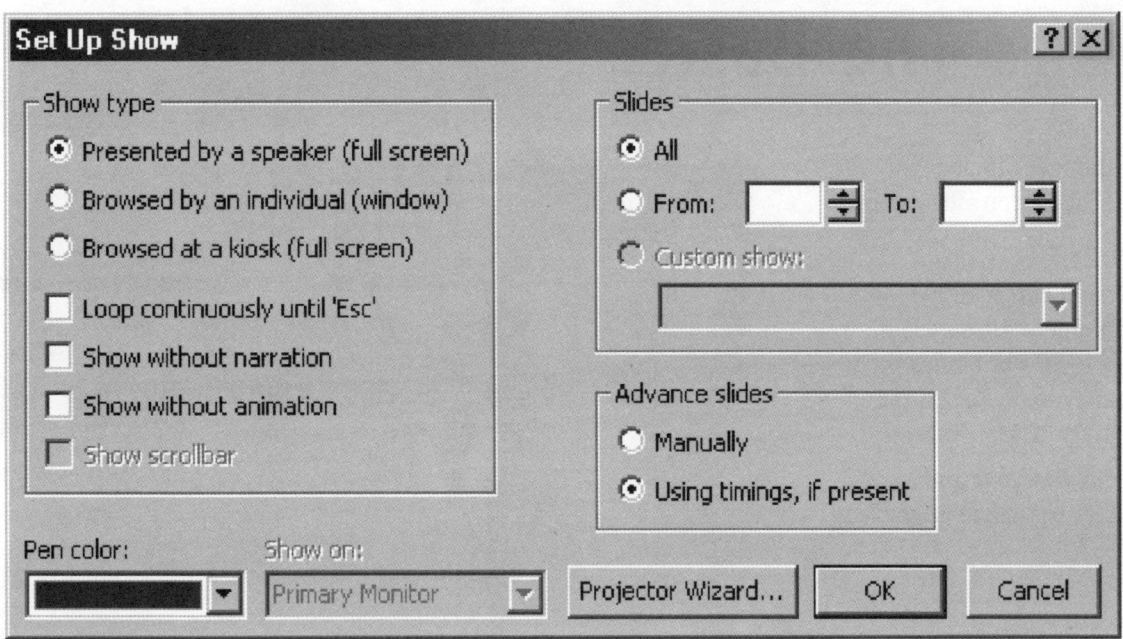

6 Ring and label with a **6** the option button you would click to make the slides advance automatically.

7 What will happen when the last slide is reached?

Answer:_____

8 Describe one situation when you might set up a kiosk presentation.

Answer: _____

_____

Answers

Sheet 1a **The Basics**

1. Lower of the main toolbars at the top of the screen (see Figure).

2. Equipment Hire

3. Click and hold cursor to the left of **Equipment Hire** and drag down to end of Slide 3 or Hold Shift key and click on the slide icons 2 and 3.

4. Choose **Edit, Delete** or press **Delete** key or press **Backspace** key.

5. See figure.

6. Slide 2.

7. Icon circled. (See figure.)

8. **Outline** View

9. **File** and then **Save**.

10. See figure.

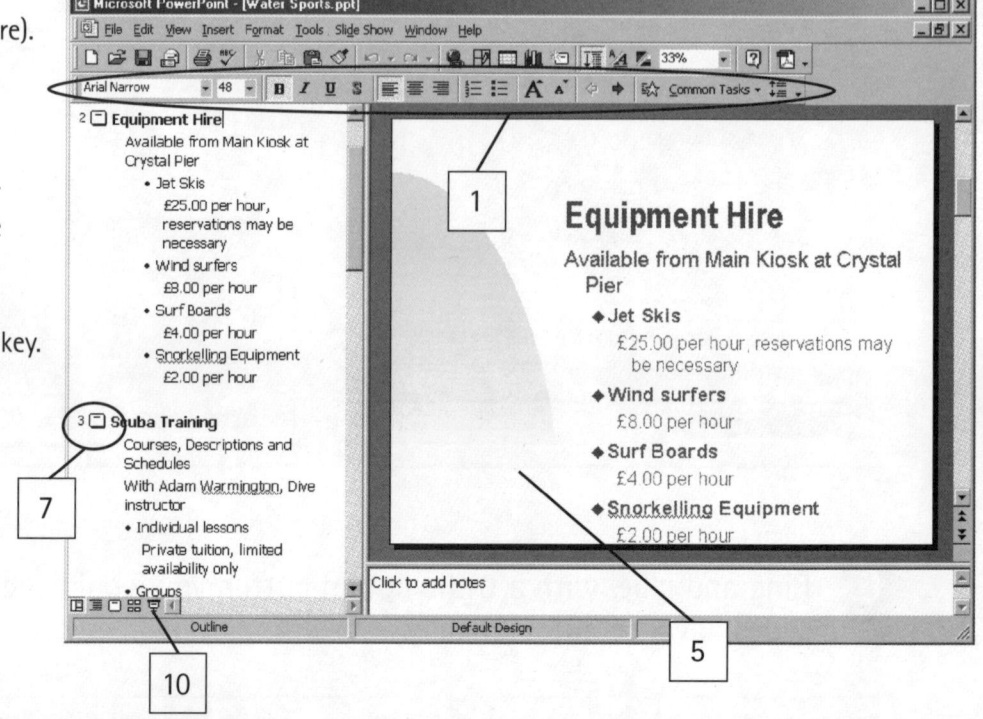

Sheet 1b **The Basics**

1. Presentation Window

2. ppt - see figure.

3. Outline View. (Accept Normal View.)

4. Change the words **EVENT NAME!!!** to **Moonwalk.**

5. Picture of an I-beam. (See figure)

6. Click at the beginning of the word **Time** and press **Enter**. Pressing Enter with the cursor at the end of EVENT NAME!!! would create another slide.

7. Luna Flares.ppt

8. **Slide Show** View button. (See figure.)

9. **Esc.**

10. See figure.

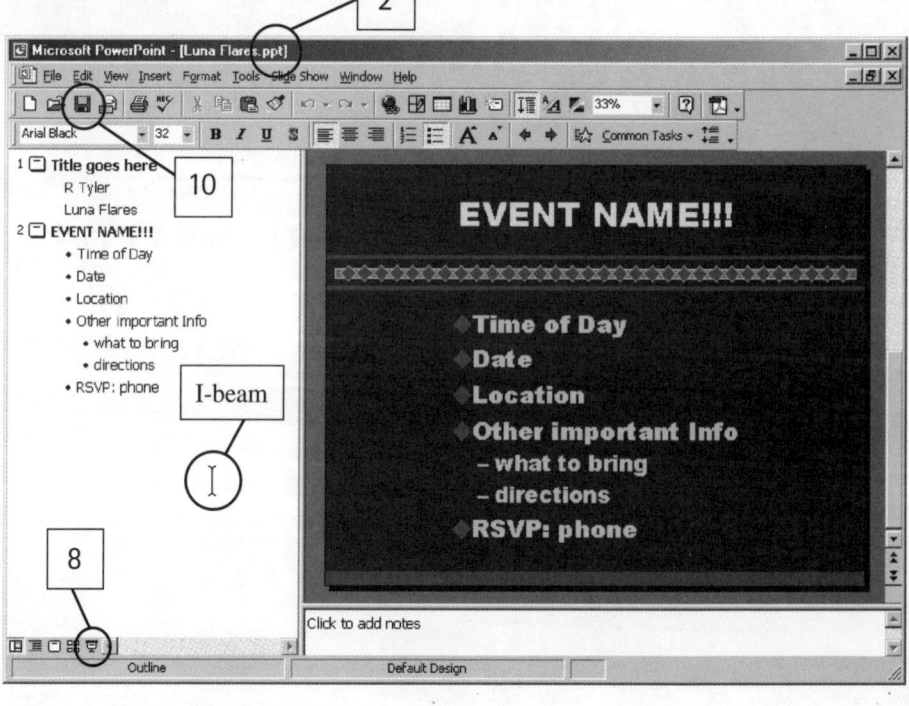

Sheet 2a Template Wizard

1. Use a title screen explaining the nature of the presentation/Not too many points on each screen/Keep points short and simple/Use sound and graphics to maintain audience attention (but sparingly!).

2. Click the title placeholder and begin typing.

3.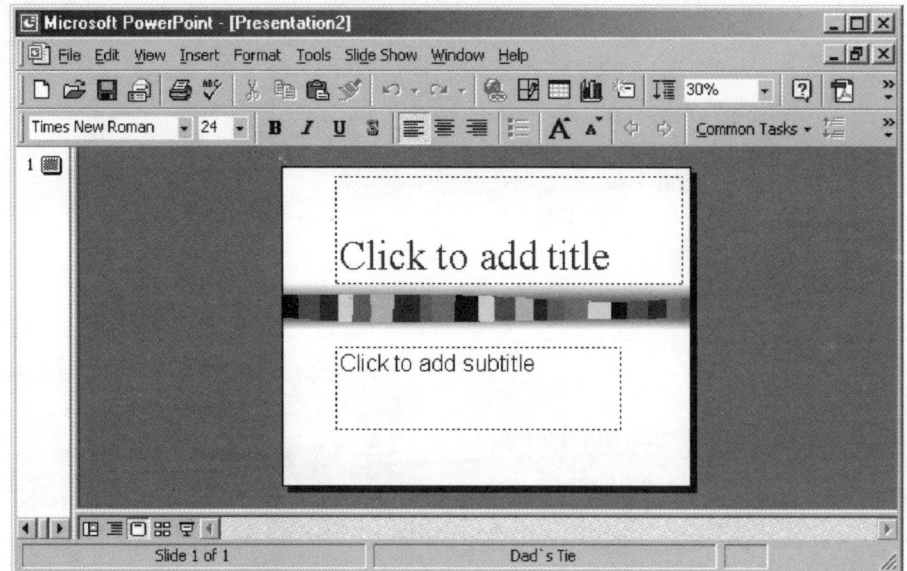

4. Select the placeholder and drag it when the pointer becomes a four-headed arrow.

5. Slide View

6. Click the **Slide Sorter** view button or select **View, Slide Sorter** from the main menu.

7.

8. The **Esc** key

9. Dads Tie.pot

10. In case you should lose your work through power failure, accidents, crashes etc. or so you can revert to a saved copy if you do something you can't undo.

Sheet 2b Template Wizard

1. Either the Title or the Sub-title. (See figure.)

2. 2 slides.

3. Select the text or select the box (i.e. make sure that the border of the placeholder is fuzzy and not striped.)

4. Click and drag the cursor over the text.

5. **Title slide** layout.

6. Use a title screen explaining the nature of the presentation/Not too many points on each screen/Keep points short and simple/ Use sound and graphics, etc.

7. (Third Image.)

8. (First Image.)

9. (Second Image.)

10. Title Slide *or* Slide number 1.

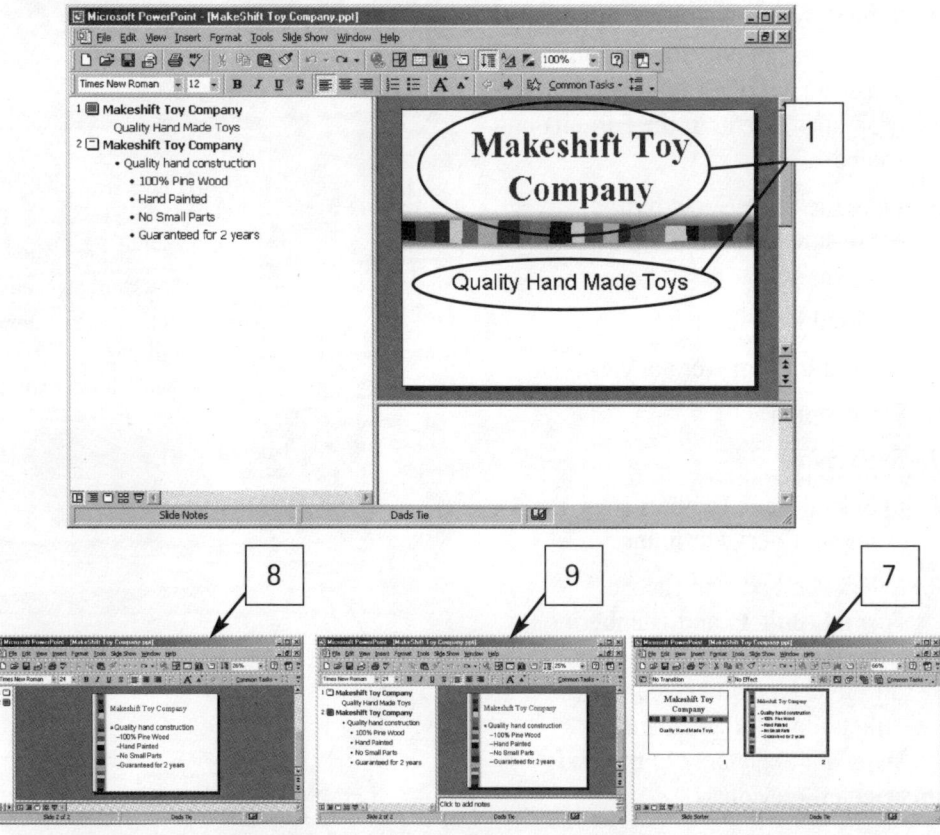

Sheet 3a **Editing a Show**

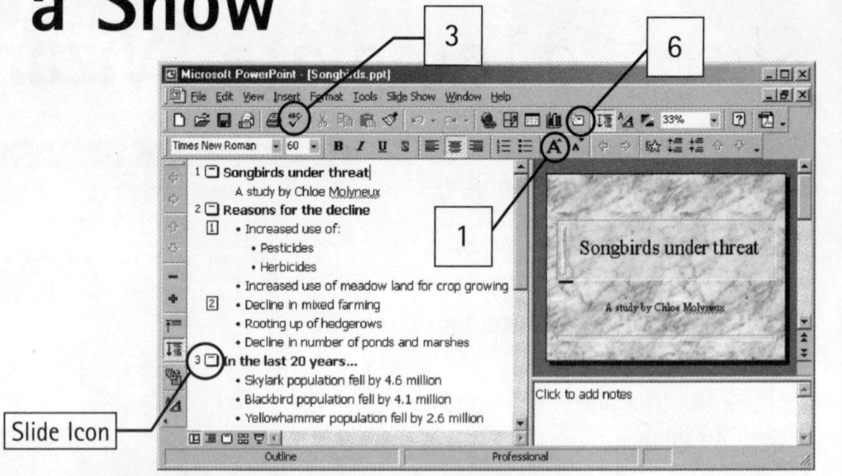

1. See figure.
2. Outline View. (Accept Normal View.)
3. See figure.
4. The **slide** icon. (See figure.)
5. Either: Click and drag slide icon 3 above slide icon 2 *or* Click and drag slide icon 2 below slide icon 3.
6. See figure.
7. The **Demote** button. (See figure.)
8. Bullets.
9. **Format, Bullets and Numbering...**
10. The status bar. (See figure.)

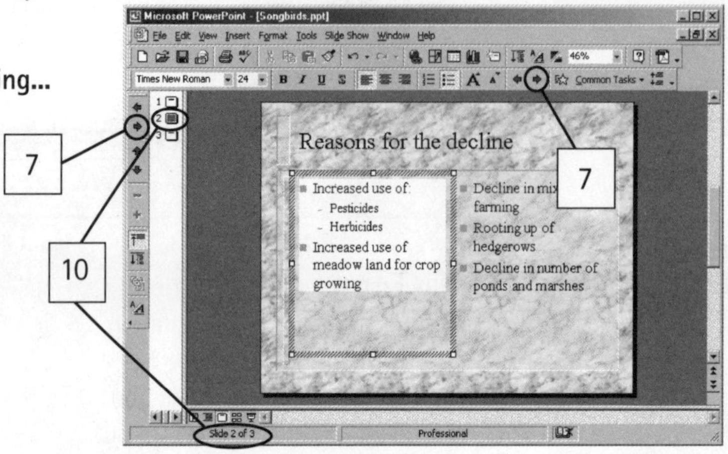

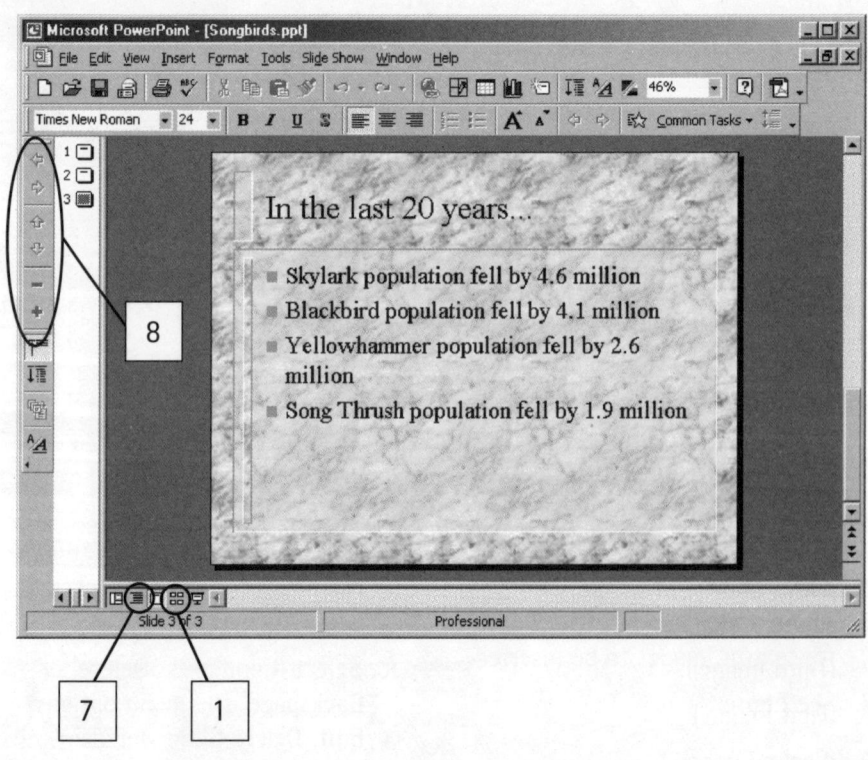

Sheet 3b **Editing a Show**

1. **Slide Sorter** view button.(See figure.)
2. Select the text and then either click the **Increase Font Size** button or select a new size from the **Font Size** drop down menu in the **Formatting** toolbar.
3. Click the **Slide Show** button. Make sure that Slide 1 is selected beforehand.
4. Bulleted List.
5. Outline View or Normal View.
6. Professional
7. See figure.
8. (b) Select **View, Toolbars** from the menu. Check **Outlining**.
9. Select the text and choose **Format, Bullets and Numbering...** from the main menu. Select a different type and colour of bullet and click **OK.** The new style will apply only to the text selected previously.

Sheet 4a **Applying Designs**

1. Slide View.

2. See figure.

3. **Apply Design Template...**

4. **Slide Color Scheme...**

5. **Apply** will apply the operation to the pre-selected slide only. **Apply to All** will apply the operation to all the slides.

6. The **Vertical Scroll** bar.

7. Select the text Ludwig van Beethoven and click the **Increase Font Size** button or select a new font size from the **Font Size** menu on the Formatting toolbar. Or select **Format, Font...** on the main menu bar.

8. Because they are **unrecognised by the PowerPoint dictionary.** They may be incorrectly spelt or unfamiliar names.

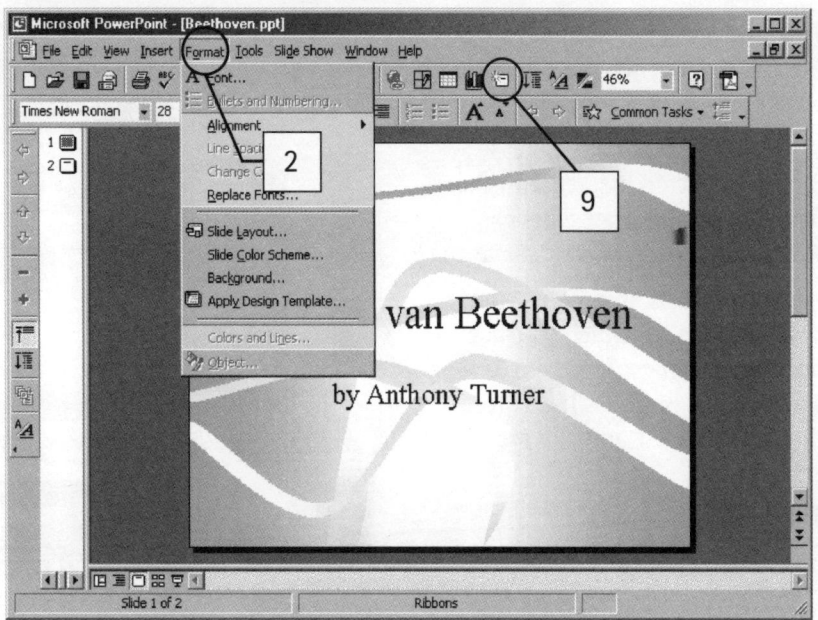

9. The **New Slide** icon.

10. Any variation on: A collection of pictures and cartoons drawn by professional artists and collected together for other people to use.

Sheet 4b **Applying Designs**

1. Slide **2**.

2. The screen would display the Slide view of Slide 1.

3. **Background...**

4. 2 of the following: Gradient, Texture, Pattern, Picture.

5. Select the slide and click **Slide Layout** from the **Format** submenu and choose a new layout.

   (The best time to do this is before you have added any text and especially before pictures have been added. The reason for this is because it will overlap new place-holders with old.)

6. An area assigned by **PowerPoint** for text or images to be inserted.

7. See figure.

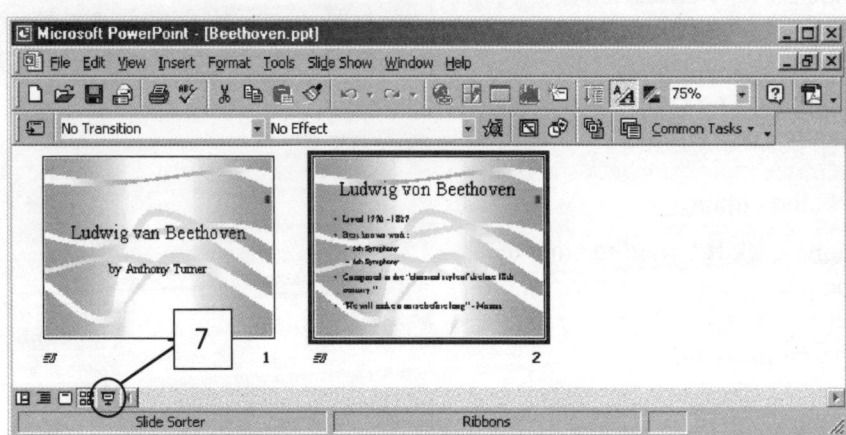

8. The **Esc** key.

9. The **Space bar** advances through the presentation and **Backspace** will move back.

10. Select it and press **Delete,** *or* **Backspace.** The menu options **Edit, Delete Slide** will also work.

Sheet 5a **Adding Objects**

1. With the cursor in the line, press the **Tab** key or click the **Demote** button.

2. Select it and press the Increase Font Size button marked 2 in the figure or use the Font Size button.

3. A placeholder is an area reserved by PowerPoint in which to place text and graphics. There are 3 placeholders on this slide. (The title, bulleted list and clip art image.)

4. See figure.

5. Double-click it.

6. Handles. They are for sizing the graphic.

7. Click and drag a corner handle.

8. 2 layouts. (See figure.)

9. 3. (Layouts 5,6 & 8 in figure.)

10. The computer could crash, power could fail, or you could do some thing you are unable to undo.

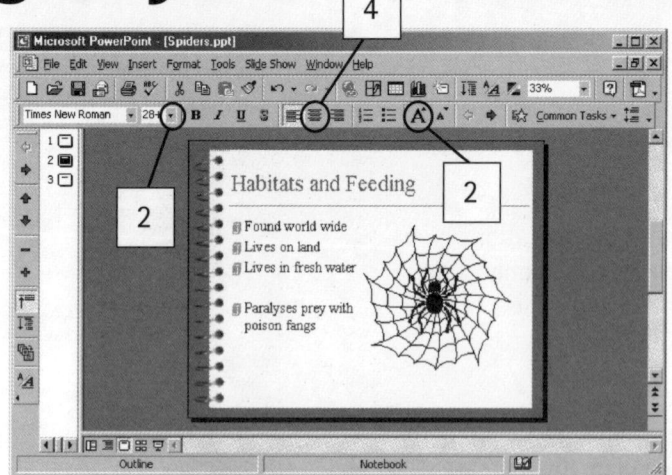

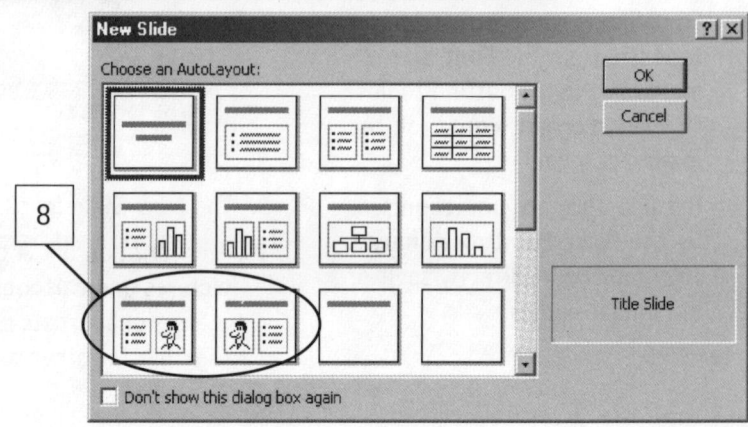

Sheet 5b **Adding Objects**

1. Slide icon 2 or 3.

2. Select the line and click on the **Bullets** button (See figure) or choose **Format, Bullet...** from the main menu and uncheck the **Use a bullet** option.

3. **Right-click** the word to bring up the pop-up menu and click **Ignore All** or use the spell checker and choose to ignore it.

4. Corner handles.

5.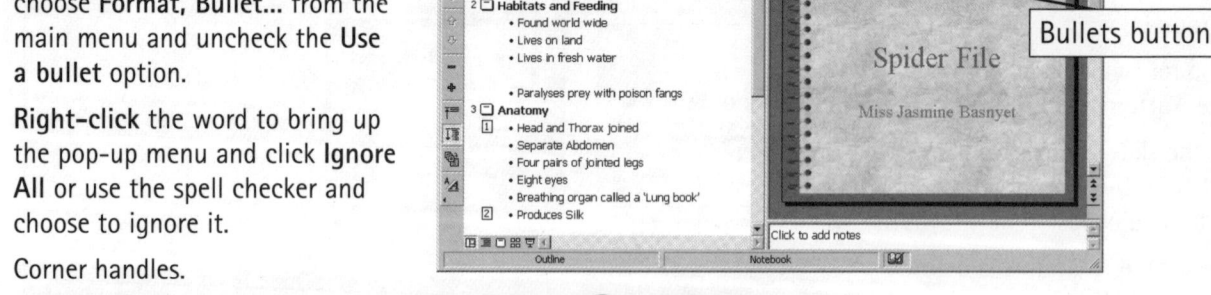

6. Drag between column headers.

7. Click on the **Column Header** and press **Delete.**

8. See figure.

9. **View, Datasheet** or **Edit, Chart Object, Edit.**

10. Click in one of the **cells** and begin typing.

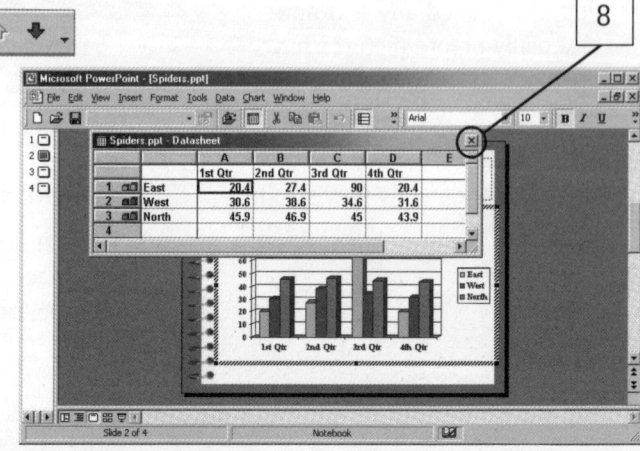

Sheet 6a **Special Effects**

1.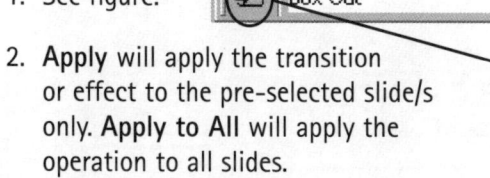

2. The **Esc** key.

3. It tells you that there is a transition applied to that slide.

4. **Box Out.**

5. Any 2 of the following: (In any direction, e.g. **Box** In or **Box** Out)

    > No Transition
    >
    > Blinds
    >
    > Box
    >
    > Checkerboard
    >
    > Cover
    >
    > Cut
    >
    > Dissolve
    >
    > Fade
    >
    > Random Bars
    >
    > Split
    >
    > Strip
    >
    > Uncover
    >
    > Wipe
    >
    > Random

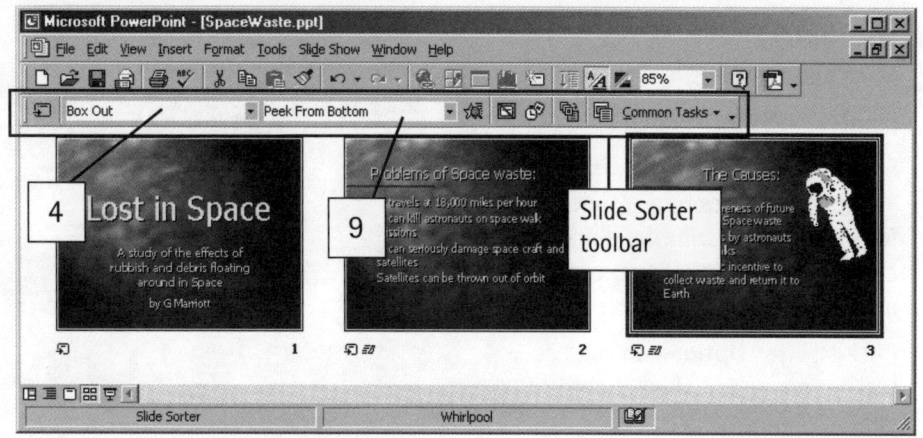

6. Peels current slide away like a set of curtains to reveal next slide underneath.

7. See figure.

8. Indicates that there is a special effect applied to that slide.

9. **Peek From Bottom.**

10. The **Space bar** and the **Backspace** key.

Sheet 6b **Special Effects**

1. See figure.

2. **Apply** will apply the transition or effect to the pre-selected slide/s only. **Apply to All** will apply the operation to all slides.

3. A **transition** will give the background screen a special action as it appears. An **effect** will give animation to the text and other objects as they appear on the screen.

4. Slides **2** and **3.**

5. Hold down the **Ctrl** key while you click on the desired slides.

6. 2. (Slides 2 and 3.)

7. **Insert, Movies and Sounds.**

8. True.

Sheet 7a **Show Time!**

1. Right-hand button.

2. **Next** and **Previous.**

3. **Pointer Options, Hidden**

4. Accept anything to assist in general explanation of a slide, for example, drawing freehand trend curves, highlighting certain points, as a pointing tool etc.

5. Click **Pointer Options** on the Pop-up menu and then choose **Pen.**

6. Click **Pointer Options** and then choose **Pen Color.**

7. Click **Screen** and then choose **Erase Pen.** (Note: moving to another screen automatically erases pen marks.)

8. Normal view, Outline view or Notes Page view (from the **View** menu).

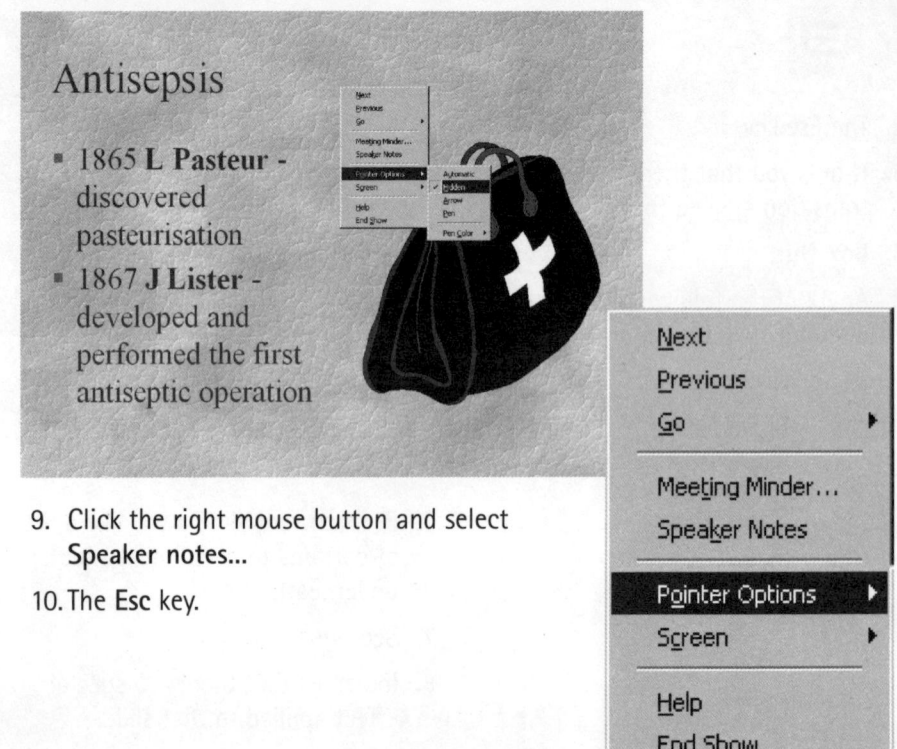

9. Click the right mouse button and select **Speaker notes...**

10. The **Esc** key.

Sheet 7b **Show Time!**

1. **Slide Show** view.

2. The Pop-up menu appears.

3. Any 3 of the following:

> Black
>
> White
>
> Red
>
> Green
>
> Blue
>
> Cyan
>
> Magenta
>
> Yellow
>
> Grey

4. **Go, By title, 3 Antisepsis.**

5. Any variations of the following:
To assist the understanding of the audience, to help them follow the presentation through, to give them something of the presentation to take with them, to make further notes on, to remind them of the points you may have made.

6. See figure.

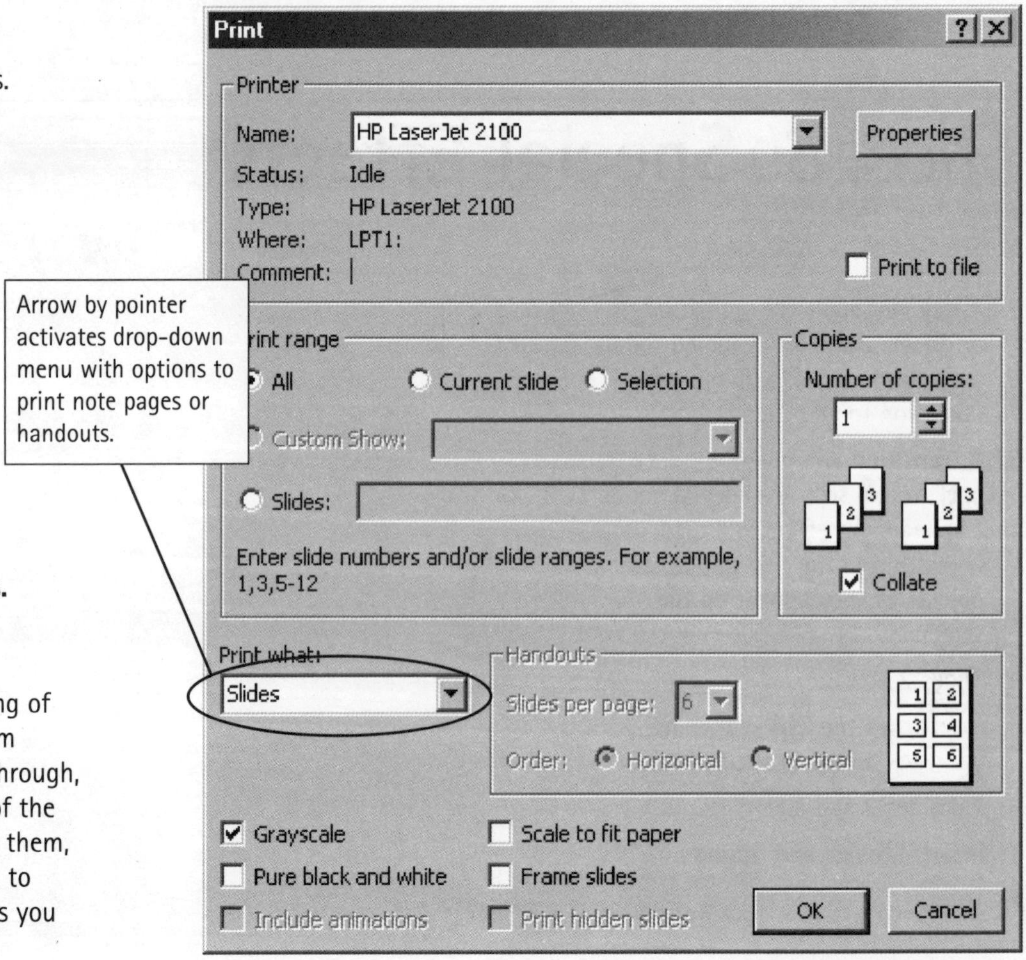

Arrow by pointer activates drop-down menu with options to print note pages or handouts.

Sheet 8a **Delivery**

1. To achieve a smoother, well-polished performance *or*

   To time the length of your presentation *or*

   To get used to speaking clearly *or*

   To help remember the points you need to make *or*

   To become more at ease with an audience.

2. Check the **hardware**.

3. Accept any of the following or variations: good eye contact or clear speech or enthusiasm or smile.

4. To keep their attention or to involve them or to help them remember your points etc.

5. Use handouts, sounds, animation or graphics.

6. Listeners tend to begin reading them during your presentation and their attention is diverted from the speaker.

Sheet 8b **Delivery**

1. Dress smartly. (Slightly smarter than your general audience is best.)

2. It is self-running.

3. See figure.

4. All the slides selected before the transition was applied.

5. See figure.

6. Either of the options shown in the second figure.

7. The presentation will loop round to the first screen again.

8. Any occasion which is likely to have many people wandering past without stopping for long, such as a school fete, an open day, parent's evening etc.

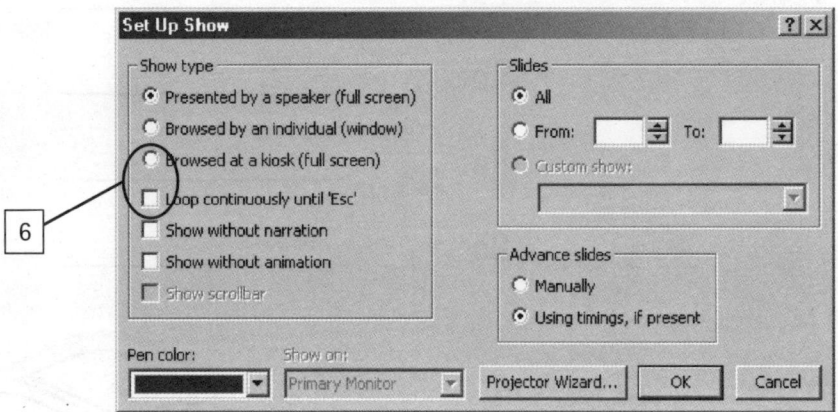

Record Sheet (Basic PowerPoint 2000)

Name: _____ Class: _____

	Sheet	Date Completed	Teacher Initials
1. The Basics	1a:	_____	_____
	1b:	_____	_____
2. Template Wizard	2a:	_____	_____
	2b:	_____	_____
3. Editing a Show	3a:	_____	_____
	3b:	_____	_____
4. Applying Designs	4a:	_____	_____
	4b:	_____	_____
5. Adding Objects	5a:	_____	_____
	5b:	_____	_____
6. Special Effects	6a:	_____	_____
	6b:	_____	_____
7. Show Time!	7a:	_____	_____
	7b:	_____	_____
8. Delivery	8a:	_____	_____
	8b:	_____	_____

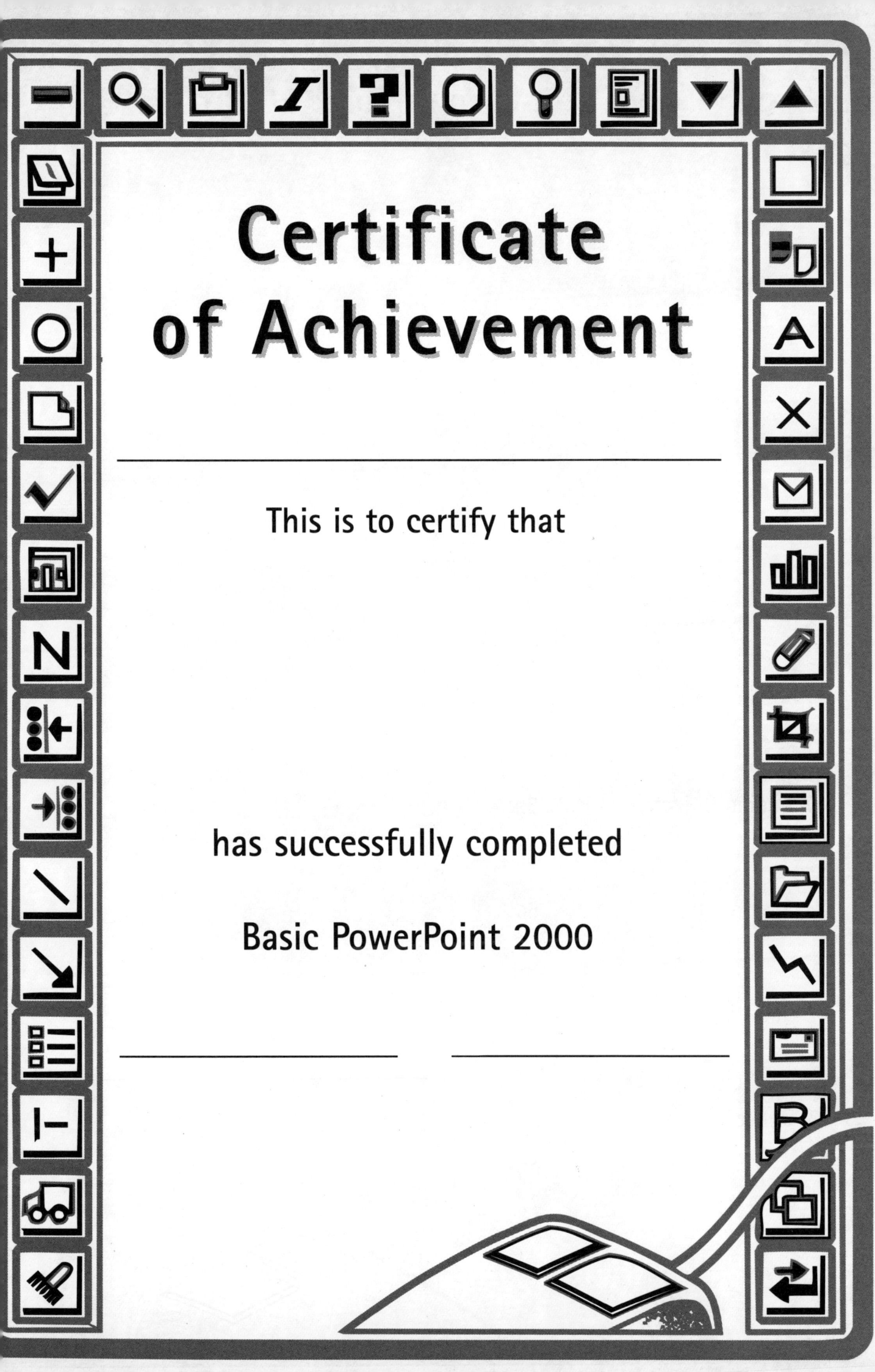

Notes

Notes